Everyday Heroes

The
Red Cross

Jill C. Wheeler
ABDO Publishing Company

visit us at
www.abdopub.com

Published by ABDO Publishing Company, 4940 Viking Drive, Edina, Minnesota 55435.
Copyright © 2003 by Abdo Consulting Group, Inc. International copyrights reserved in all countries. No part of this book may be reproduced in any form without written permission from the publisher.

Printed in the United States.

Editors: Kate A. Conley, Stephanie Hedlund, Kristianne E. Vieregger
Photo Credits: AP/Wide World, The Canadian Press, Corbis, TimePix
Art Direction: Neil Klinepier

Library of Congress Cataloging-in-Publication Data

Wheeler, Jill C., 1964-
    The Red Cross / Jill C. Wheeler.
        p. cm. -- (Everyday heroes)
    Includes index.
    Contents: Haunted by suffering -- An idea takes hold -- The movement spreads -- The American Red Cross in action -- Many needs, many jobs -- The Canadian Red Cross at work -- When disaster strikes -- The Red Cross around the world -- Do your part.
    ISBN 1-57765-857-4
    1. Red Cross--Juvenile literature. 2. Disaster relief--Juvenile literature. [1. Red Cross. 2. Voluntarism. 3. Disaster relief.] I. Title. II. Everyday heroes (Edina, Minn.)

HV568 .W48 2002
361.7'7--dc21
                                                                        2002071238

Contents

Haunted by Suffering 4

An Idea Takes Hold 6

The Movement Spreads 10

Working Together 14

American Red Cross 16

Canadian Red Cross 22

Do Your Part 28

Glossary 30

Web Sites 31

Index 32

Haunted by Suffering

On June 24, 1859, Swiss banker Henry Dunant (doo-NAHN) traveled to Solferino, Italy. Earlier that day, Solferino had been the site of a major battle. More than 40,000 soldiers lay on the battlefield.

The wounded soldiers had lain for hours without food, water, or medical attention. Dunant wanted to help them. So he asked some local women and other travelers to help him give aid. They gave the soldiers water and **dressed** their wounds.

Dunant worked nonstop for three days. He saved many lives. Yet many more soldiers died because they had not been helped soon enough.

When Dunant returned to his home in Switzerland, he wrote a book

Henry Dunant

called *A Memory of Solferino*. In it, he described the suffering during and after the battle. Then he suggested forming relief societies of trained volunteers. They would aid wounded soldiers.

The Battle of Solferino

An Idea Takes Hold

Dunant's book was successful. Soon, Dunant and four other men formed a committee to put the volunteer idea into action. This committee later became the International Committee of the Red Cross (ICRC).

In 1863, delegates from several nations met with the committee in Geneva, Switzerland. They agreed that volunteers should be allowed to aid wounded soldiers. They also agreed that the volunteers must be **neutral**.

The delegates wanted a symbol for their organization. They chose a red cross on a white background. It was Switzerland's flag with the colors reversed. Switzerland was a neutral country. The delegates hoped the symbol would remind people that the volunteers were neutral as well.

Opposite page: The five founding members of the ICRC

Général G.H. Dufour

Gustave Moynier

Henry Dunant

Dr Louis Appia

Dr Th. Maunoir

Comité internat! Fondateur
de l'oeuvre de la Croix-Rouge
• GENÈVE, 1863 •

In 1864, the committee met again. At the meeting, delegates from 12 nations signed the Geneva Convention. This treaty was a set of rules for proper conduct during war. It explained how to treat wounded soldiers and medical workers. These rules were called **humanitarian** laws.

The Geneva Conventions

Today, there are four Geneva Conventions. They were formally adopted on August 12, 1949. All four conventions call for humane treatment of people during conflicts.

Nearly every nation in the world has agreed to honor the Geneva Conventions. Government and military officials can be punished if they violate these treaties.

The four Geneva Conventions seek humane treatment for:
- *wounded and sick soldiers on the battlefield, as well as those aiding them*
- *wounded, sick, or shipwrecked soldiers at sea*
- *prisoners of war*
- *civilians during wartime*

Delegates discuss the first Geneva Convention in 1864.

The Red Cross had its first test in 1870. That year, the **Franco-Prussian War** began. As at Solferino, many people were injured. This time, however, Red Cross volunteers aided the wounded soldiers.

An American **relief worker** named Clara Barton volunteered in the Franco-Prussian War. During the war, Barton learned about the Red Cross Movement. She decided to bring the Movement to the United States.

Clara Barton volunteers with the Red Cross in Strasbourg, France, during the Franco-Prussian War.

The Movement Spreads

Clara Barton had been a **relief worker** during the U.S. **Civil War**. Like Dunant, she had witnessed terrible suffering. After the **Franco-Prussian War**, she returned to the United States. She worked to begin an American Red Cross Society.

Any nation that wanted a Red Cross Society first had to sign the Geneva Convention. The United States had not signed this treaty. Despite that, Barton founded the American Association of the Red Cross in May 1881.

Barton's young organization had its first job that summer. Volunteers traveled to Michigan to aid the victims of forest fires. They brought tools, clothing, and money. They helped the fire victims recover and rebuild.

Meanwhile, Barton **lobbied** the U.S. government to sign the Geneva Convention. In March 1882, the government finally signed the treaty. This made the American Red Cross official.

Clara Barton

11

Dr. George S. Ryerson founded the Canadian Red Cross in 1885. It started when he helped Canadian soldiers during the **North West Rebellion**. During this conflict, Ryerson used a wagon to carry wounded soldiers.

Unfortunately, Ryerson's wagon looked like the other army wagons. He needed a way to tell soldiers not to attack his wagon. So he flew a Red Cross flag over it.

Meanwhile, Red Cross Societies were organized in other parts of the world. In some **Muslim** countries, people disliked the organization's symbol. They thought the red cross was a symbol of Christianity. So they began using a red **crescent** on a white background instead. Many Muslim countries still use this symbol.

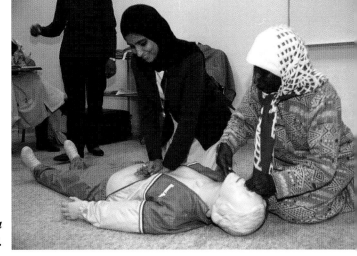

Women practice their first aid skills at a Red Crescent training center in Kuwait.

Today, the Red Cross and Red **Crescent** Movement has operations in nearly 180 countries. It is the world's largest **humanitarian** network. More than 100 million people volunteer with the Movement.

The Red Cross and Red Crescent Movement's symbols

Working Together

The Red Cross and Red **Crescent** Movement works in almost every country. The Movement has three parts. They are the ICRC, the National Societies, and the International Federation of Red Cross and Red Crescent Societies.

The ICRC is the founding body of the Red Cross Movement. The ICRC's mission is to protect the lives and **dignity** of people affected by war and violence. It **coordinates** the Movement's work in situations of conflict. It also grants official recognition to the National Societies.

National Societies aid public officials in their home countries. Every country offers different services to meet its people's needs. For example, national societies may offer **disaster** relief services and health programs. During wars, national societies aid civilians and soldiers.

The International Federation of Red Cross and Red Crescent Societies helps the National Societies work together. It also coordinates relief efforts for international disasters.

Opposite page: A Spanish Red Cross volunteer stands near boxes of emergency aid that will be shipped to Afghanistan.

The Fundamental Principles

Seven fundamental principles guide the Red Cross and Red Crescent Movement. They are:

<u>Humanity</u> – *the Movement works to prevent and relieve human suffering.*

<u>Impartiality</u> – *the Movement works to relieve suffering no matter a person's race, religion, class, or nationality.*

<u>Neutrality</u> – *the Movement may not take sides in any conflict.*

<u>Independence</u> – *the Movement's National Societies must remain separate from their governments.*

<u>Voluntary Service</u> – *service in the Movement is by choice and without any desire for gain.*

<u>Unity</u> – *each country can have only one Red Cross or Red Crescent Society, and it must be open to all.*

<u>Universality</u> – *the Movement is worldwide and all National Societies share equal responsibility in aiding each other.*

American Red Cross

Today, the American Red Cross is the largest **humanitarian agency** in the United States. It has 1,100 chapters and more than 1 million volunteers. Ninety-seven percent of all American Red Cross workers are volunteers.

All kinds of people volunteer for the American Red Cross. Almost half of them are under age 25. Volunteers receive different training depending on their jobs. Some use skills they already have, such as nursing, teaching, or engineering. Others learn their skills through Red Cross training programs.

The American Red Cross uses a computer **database** to match volunteers to openings. Some volunteers may help with only one event. Others may volunteer for years. Volunteers also govern the organization. They provide management and support positions, too.

The U.S. **Congress** granted the American Red Cross authority to provide **disaster** relief in 1905. Today, the

An American Red Cross volunteer checks the message board at a shelter set up for victims of a wildfire.

American Red Cross responds to more than 67,000 **disasters** each year. These include natural disasters such as fires, floods, hurricanes, tornadoes, and earthquakes. The American Red Cross also responds to train crashes, explosions, and **hazardous** material spills.

The American Red Cross helps communities in other ways, too. Its blood drives collect half of the nation's blood supply. It also provides almost one-fifth of the nation's **donated tissue**. The American Red Cross assists with lifesaving medical research as well.

Additionally, American Red Cross volunteers train more than 11 million people in health and safety skills each year. Volunteers teach classes on **first aid**, **CPR**, baby-sitting, swimming, water safety, and AIDS.

Students participate in a Red Cross lifeguarding program.

American Red Cross volunteers provide other services, too. Some volunteers help people plan for **disasters**. Other volunteers help people with their day-to-day needs. They may provide transportation, meals, homeless shelters, and **latchkey** programs.

Victims of a California earthquake wait in line to receive supplies from the American Red Cross.

The American Red Cross also works with other National Societies and their volunteers outside the United States. Volunteers help with **disaster** response, health care, food programs, and message delivery. In addition, the volunteers promote international **humanitarian** laws in other nations.

A Red Cross volunteer and a state police officer work together to help a woman whose home was hit by a tornado.

Though the American Red Cross is not part of the government, it often works with federal **agencies** and state and local governments. For example, the American Red Cross often works with the Federal Emergency Management Agency (FEMA). Both the Red Cross and FEMA are usually available when large **disasters** strike.

Since the American Red Cross is not part of the government, it does not receive tax money for funding. Instead, it relies on **donations** from businesses and individuals.

In turn, the American Red Cross and other National Societies donate money to the ICRC. These donations, along with donations made by other organizations, help fund the ICRC.

Aiding the Military

The American Red Cross has a long history of aiding the military during times of war. The first time the American Red Cross aided the military was in the Spanish-American War of 1898.

During World Wars I and II, the American Red Cross organized nurses and hospitals to aid wounded soldiers. It also operated canteens that provided food and drinks to soldiers who were on the front lines.

During the Korean War and the Vietnam War, American Red Cross workers collected blood for wounded soldiers. When soldiers returned to the United States, Red Cross workers helped them adjust to civilian life.

In the Persian Gulf War, Red Cross workers relayed emergency messages and provided humanitarian aid. Today, American Red Cross workers continue to aid U.S. soldiers stationed throughout the world.

Canadian Red Cross

The Canadian Red Cross first operated as a branch of the British Red Cross. In 1909, Canada's government passed the Canadian Red Cross Society Act. It authorized the Red Cross to provide volunteer aid throughout Canada. In 1927, the ICRC recognized the Canadian Red Cross as an independent organization.

The Canadian Red Cross is not a government **agency**. However, it works with government agencies when necessary. Red Cross volunteers also work with other relief agencies, businesses, and community groups.

The Canadian Red Cross is responsible for its own funding. It relies on **donations**. Many individuals and businesses donate money to the Canadian Red Cross.

Opposite page: A Canadian Red Cross volunteer sits at a donation table before a Calgary Flames game.

Canadian Red Cross volunteers are active in Canada and around the world. They help people in many situations. Canadian Red Cross volunteers help people whose survival, safety, security, well-being, or **dignity** is threatened.

The Canadian Red Cross trains thousands of volunteers each year. They learn how to respond to emergencies and **disasters**. For example, some volunteers learn how to manage temporary shelters for victims. Others learn to operate a computer system that helps victims find their families.

Some volunteers also work behind the scenes to make relief efforts possible. Volunteers do accounting work, operate computer **databases**, manage warehouses, and schedule other volunteers. Whatever talents a person has, the Red Cross can use them.

The Red Cross offers many services to Canadian communities. For example, the Canadian Red Cross has seven different programs for **first aid**. These programs

Canadian Red Cross volunteers prepare temporary beds for travelers who were stranded after American airports were temporarily closed due to the terrorist attacks of September 11, 2001.

train about 300,000 people each year. Training ranges from baby-sitting basics to emergency first response.

Water safety is also important to the Canadian Red Cross. Red Cross water-safety volunteers teach more than 1 million Canadians each year. Volunteers teach swimming and water-safety rules. They urge boaters to wear life jackets and teach people about safety on ice. Fewer Canadians drown today than 50 years ago thanks to the Red Cross.

Additionally, the Canadian Red Cross prepares people for **disasters**. It also works to prevent them. But when disasters do strike, Red Cross volunteers are there to help.

Canadian Red Cross volunteers work in two phases, called relief and recovery. The relief phase happens immediately after a disaster. Volunteers help local governments provide immediate, basic needs for victims. These include **first aid**, food, shelter, and clothing. Disasters can be sad or frightening, so volunteers also provide victims with emotional support.

Next, the recovery phase begins. In recovery, Red Cross volunteers continue to aid victims. They may help victims find new homes. In addition, volunteers may help victims get what they need to return to work or school. Red Cross volunteers also find other resources that victims may need.

This family spent the night at a Red Cross shelter in Montreal after ice storms shut down highways and toppled power lines across eastern Canada.

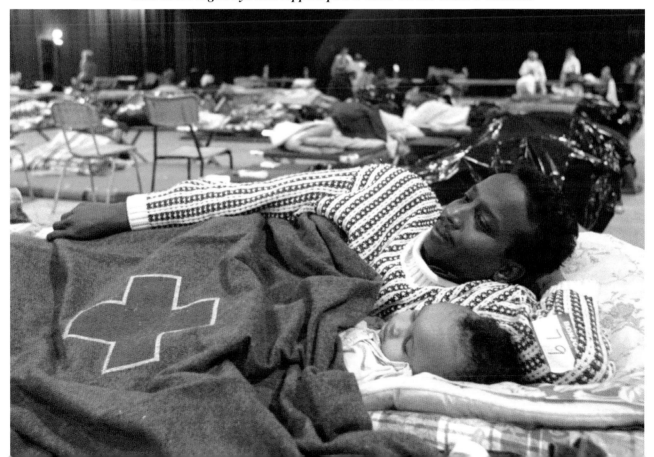

Do Your Part

Anyone can make a difference by being prepared. Here are some ideas on what you can do to help:

- Take a Red Cross baby-sitting class. Having the proper skills will prepare you to help a child you are watching in the event of an emergency.
- Learn how to be a lifeguard. Learning to swim is very important. By being a lifeguard, you might save someone from drowning.
- Create a **disaster** plan for your family. Knowing where to go and who to contact after a disaster could save somebody's life.
- Ask your parents to volunteer with you for your local Red Cross chapter. Becoming involved in your community will not only help other people, it will also make you feel proud of what you can do!

An instructor helps students carry a row boat into the water. They are learning boating skills as part of a Red Cross summer camp.

Glossary

agency - a department of the government.

civil war - a war between groups in the same country. The United States of America and the Confederate States of America fought a civil war from 1861 to 1865.

Congress - the lawmaking body of the United States. It is made up of the Senate and the House of Representatives. It meets in Washington, D.C.

coordinate - to bring into a common action or movement.

CPR - stands for cardiopulmonary resuscitation. It is an emergency lifesaving method in which someone tries to restart a patient's heart and lungs.

crescent - the shape of the moon when it is small and thin.

database - a large collection of information.

dignity - the quality of being proud and having self-respect.

disaster - an event that causes suffering or loss of life.

donate - to give.

dress - to apply a dressing, such as a bandage or gauze, to a wound.

first aid - emergency care given to a person before regular medical care is available.

Franco-Prussian War - 1870 to 1871. A war fought between France and Prussia, a former kingdom in Germany.

hazardous - involving danger or risk.

humanitarian - concerning the general welfare of human beings.

latchkey - of or relating to a child who must spend part of the day unsupervised because his or her parents are at work.

lobby - to influence lawmakers to vote a certain way.

Muslim - a person who follows Islam. It is a religion based on the teachings of Muhammad as they appear in the Koran.

neutral - not taking sides in a conflict.

North West Rebellion - an 1885 conflict over land. The conflict was between the Canadian government and the Métis, people who were part white and part Native American. The Métis were defeated.

relief worker - a person who helps others in painful or difficult situations.

tissue - a group of cells that works together to perform the same job.

Web Sites

Would you like to learn more about the Red Cross and Red Crescent Movement? Please visit **www.abdopub.com** to find up-to-date Web site links about Red Cross history, services the Red Cross provides, and ways to volunteer in your community. These links are routinely monitored and updated to provide the most current information available.

Index

A

American Association of
    the Red Cross 10
American Red Cross 10,
    16, 18, 19, 20, 21

B

Barton, Clara 9, 10
British Red Cross 22

C

Canada 12, 22, 24, 26
Canadian Red Cross 12,
    22, 24, 26, 27
Canadian Red Cross
    Society Act 22
Civil War, U.S. 10
Congress, U.S. 16

D

disaster relief 10, 14, 16,
    18, 19, 20, 24, 26, 27
Dunant, Henry 4, 5, 6,
    10

F

Federal Emergency
    Management
    Agency 21
Franco-Prussian War 9,
    10
funding 21, 22

G

Geneva Convention 8,
    10
Geneva, Switzerland 6

H

humanitarian laws 8, 20

I

International Committee
    of the Red Cross 6,
    8, 14, 21, 22
International Federation
    of Red Cross and
    Red Crescent
    Societies 14
Italy 4

M

Memory of Solferino, A
    5, 6
Michigan 10

N

National Societies 10,
    12, 14, 20, 21
North West Rebellion 12

R

Red Cross and Red
    Crescent Movement
    9, 13, 14
Ryerson, George S. 12

S

safety tips 28
Solferino, Italy 4, 9
Switzerland 4, 6

U

United States 9, 10, 16,
    18, 19, 20, 21

V

volunteer training 16, 24